Let Me Tell You...

Ileili R. Tahauri

Order this book online at www.trafford.com
or email orders@trafford.com

Most Trafford titles are also available at major online book retailers.

Printed in the United States of America.

ISBN: 978-1-4269-1393-8 (sc)

*Our mission is to efficiently provide the world's finest, most comprehensive book publishing
service, enabling every author to experience success. To find out how to publish your book,
your way, and have it available worldwide, visit us online at www.trafford.com*

Trafford rev. 09/01/2010

Trafford
PUBLISHING www.trafford.com

North America & international
toll-free: 1 888 232 4444 (USA & Canada)
phone: 250 383 6864 ✦ fax: 812 355 4082

Dedication:

"For my mother, Jill.
Thank you for encouraging me to turn
my passion into a career. This is just the beginning.
This is the opportunity you've provided me with
and I will gladly take it and run with it.
Here's to many more pages
to be written."

There is no greater agony than bearing an untold story inside you."
-Maya Angelou

Acknowledgments

I'd like to thank the adults first for being my inspiration. Thank you mom for making this publication possible. Thank you Uncle Daniel for using your publishing experience to help me with this summer project that turned into a year. I am so grateful for your faith in me and inspiring me to go through with publishing my own works. Taking time from your busy schedule to help me understand the whole process meant so much to me! Thank you to the Kamehameha Schools Maui Campus staff: Ms. Ka`awa for never giving up on me. My favorite intermediate educators Mrs. Damuni and Mrs. Kapisi for tolerating me and the consistent push for better. Also Mr. Cagasan, who was there when I first decided writing should be my profession. Thank you Jessica Pearl for giving me the best job I've ever had and encouraging me to go to college and get my work out there. As for the people in my generation, thank you goes to my closest friends whom I always gave my rough drafts to during class, lunch, or on the bus. Nadine, Serena, Malia, Sierra, and Wila. I appreciate that you all stuck by me and my mood swings and openly read what I had to write. Thank you Huali for helping me expand my style of writing. Thank you Corinne and Pele for also being willing to read my work. Thank you Mercedes for knowing the value of a first draft and being the most awesome love and support a cousin could ask for! Thank you Terani for being the first person to tell me I could be an author if I wanted to. You helped me realize I could be anything I aspired to be, it just takes time. Huge thank you goes to Jarren for giving me such honest and positive reviews. Your critique was of the most value because of you did so in such a professional manner. I couldn't be more thankful, Panda. Last but not least, mahalo to Sylvia for taking the time to be there for me and understanding that poetry is therapeutic for me and being willing to read and be there for me. I'm not sure I would've survived my first semester in college without you. All these people surely had positive influences on me and the way I wrote. I thankyou all very much. I wouldn't have gotten this far if it weren't for the support I got from each of you throughout the years.

Foreword

As most of you know, this book was supposed to be printed over a year ago. My procrastination got the best of me after the first proof came back because I'm too lazy to sit still and revise the entire thing. But I've finally done it! In a sense at least. Although I had a few different directions for this book, I've had a couple people convince me that every author's first publishing is a tad imperfect. Of course, being that it's my first book I had very high expectations of it and wanted every punctuation mark, name, photos, and placement strictly in their designated areas. But as reality set in, my mother was right. The longer I hold on to a project, the more I will want to change it as time progresses. She was right when she said that I was a different person when I started this book, as when I've finished it. I have different thoughts, new ideas, more 'improvements' if you will. But people need to see the original; what I saw when I first started. Also, my cousin Mercedes was wise in telling me not to change one thing about it. She asked that I left everything exactly the way it was because she didn't want to miss anything; she didn't want me to leave a single thing out. She knows me well enough to realize I definitely would have changed a lot of the manuscript, had I had my way. So I've come to the conclusion that if anything can be salvaged from my poetry, any lessons or raw, school-girl feelings that can be found, should indeed be left as is, specifically for her. And for everyone else her age, I'd be so happy if they can relate. They don't even have to like it, just know exactly where I'm coming from. After all, this is only the beginning.

Contents

Key Players:

"I know God won't give me anything I can't handle. I just wish he didn't trust me so much."-Mother Teresa

Living & Breathing:

"If the world hates you, keep in mind that it hated me first."- John 15:18

Heartache:

"People will forget what you said. People will forget what you did. But people will never forget how you made them feel."- Maya Angelou

Key Players:

"I know God won't give me anything I can't handle. I just wish he didn't trust me so much."-Mother Teresa

Dad?

Do you ever smell a memory? Something that throws you in the past?
And when you finally get there, you wish it would forever last?
I had that feeling today as I woke up & smelled cologne
Thinking, "dad's up getting ready for work" to find I'm all alone.
Nothing like that after shave, a strong whiff in the air
Reminding me of those happy days, when my dad was really there
He'd wake up before the sun, shower & start the day
Then I'd get up around 6 & beg him just to stay
A daily routine to spend time with dad so frequently denied
I'd always end up crying but cease the sadness he has tried
I'd break things & spill them, all over the kitchen floor
Just so he'd clean it up, & stay a few minutes more
Today the past grabbed hold of me, & man did it hug me fast
Cause never did I long so bad, to be back in my past
The days when I enjoyed home life, seeing my dad every day
Unlike now I dread this house; I prolong it in every way
Going home is like a chore, this house holds me no joy
Seems like it's just me, cause it's a different story if you're a boy
No curfew no boundaries, no mile-long lists of "to do's"
No time to sleep in or relax, no time to simply cruise
Back in the days when my dad was here it seemed there were no rules
But now he's gone & I'm stuck here, with a bunch of stupid fools
I miss those ironed outfits; all laid out nicely to go get paid
Man when my dad was here, we really had it made
I didn't have to go to church, football was always on TV
I could go where I want & do things I like, dad just let me BE
Yeah I guess I was a daddy's girl, it's gonna stick with me for a while
But until it wears off I'm in this house, wishing I was I was still a
child

No Kin To Me

She must not be your sister
I see no resemblance
A familiar face is all we recognize
No kin to you, oh "solitary one"
You're just too damn good.
What lucky parents you must have,
that bore such a righteous boy
They're so proud.
And look, you're famous beyond your district
what a privilege it must be
Everybody knows your name.
An only child? But of course!
He travels alone, no ties.
Just his mother who loves him so well.
Who's that girl? Oh right...
That's what's-her-face, I heard of her.
How strange her presence seems.
He invades her home and eats her food
Her friends are well aware of who he is
But he fails to acknowledge.
What a shame,
I don't even know you.
She's careful not to shake your perfect world!
Only your essentials know why she's here.
Your unfortunate relations?
World, stop revolving! They share parents??!
How tragic that must be... for him.
Indeed-
She's never asked for special treatment

I don't hold the significance of a diamond.
However, sir,
A sibling wouldn't hurt.
But I don't even know you.

I'm Not Savable

I understand what you have felt
The night you saw me drop
Never in a million years
would I ask you to witness such a sight
It must have been heart wrenching
To see your friend go down without a fight
But I understand why you sat there
Not a sound, just an apologetic glance
The anxiety, the fear, the the utter repulsion
How I wish you were somewhere else
A place the guilt and indecision couldn't catch you
A place your eyes were at peace
I wished the blind hatred never saw you sitting pretty
That their disgusting intentions never knew you existed
An apology for a friend for hafting to endure that
To see me exposed, vulnerable, at my lowest point.
Drunken and bruised and high as a kite,
Crawling on the asphalt like a piece of trash.
I understand the rush of air to the membrane
What to do, think, or say? Scream if you may?
I'd never ask a friend to put their self in harm's way
Not on my account.

We're Done

As stoned as a boulder that's been blown to pieces,
As fattening as sweets, just like the Reeses,
As loving as an aunty with a bunch of nieces,
As torn as a picture that's been ripped to pieces.
I'm changing my ways & I'm changing it fast
Once my move is made, it better last
The fuck ups, the shut ups, the suck ups galore
Overflowing this island right up to our shore
Tired of droning & hearing your voice
Tired of never being given a choice
The silence to violence in this lovely corrupted place
Pissing me off with every slap in the face
Used & abused, owned & neglected
Finally your bullshit is easily rejected
Running my life cause you couldn't control yours
Too fucking lazy to do your own chores
Slave girl, skank, damn bitch, prostitution,
Every accusation from your pathetic delusion
As broke as a busted lock on a door
As down as a beat up kid of the floor
As fed up as a girl being pressured for more
As done with you as I've ever been before.

You Couldn't Wait

I didn't like you much but I think I could've saved you
God knows you're soul is sorry. Trust me, I've been there too
I don't doubt you were a good man but what you did left behind a
mess
If I knew I could've helped you passed by far you're hardest test
I'm sorry I paid no attention; obviously you were more at risk
If I knew you needed guidance, you would've been the top of my list
You knew not to be selfish but you left behind three brothers
My mom is now a first time widow; I bet you'll hear it from your
mother
Did it really work, this escape that you planned?
Was what you did worth it, taking your life with your own hand...?
No doubt, you will be missed. I saw you lying cold, calm and pale
But you were better than that, now lives are left bitter and stale
You thought you did yourself a favor. I could've done that but so
much more
Even though I didn't like you much, you would've seen me walk
through that door
I recognized you on that level, not quite elder but definitely no teen
I didn't like you much but our thought levels were in between
I refuse to drop my head; my palms are no place to cry
I can hold out till they all pull through, until then my tears are dry

I hope you're happier where ever you've gone,
Our noses are pink and our eyes to the sky.
Expressions blown apart...
And we'll always be wondering why.

Living & Breathing:

"If the world hates you, keep in mind that it hated me first."- John 15:18

We Come In 2's

Secrets don't make friends,
However, this I know...
Imaginary friends resemble secrets
They remain, as long as you can entertain it
Should you slip into a bore,
you realize someone's missing
Beside yourself in an empty room,
the only body heat is your own under stiff sheets,
and your voice is the only one heard.
Secrets are a heavy burden
no matter how insignificant they seem.
But I'd rather not.
It's like walking in the dark
Never sure where your feet lead you
They manipulate your intentions
they sabotage your disposition
Your smile must avert attention from leaky eyes
Fighting back every impulse
To shout what you really meant
To reach out, skin on skin comfort
To gaze without caution
To cling for dear life, preventing an exit
Secrets are a crafty business
Personalizing a habit, a hidden truth, a craving
What punishment it is enough,
having to assume the role
Revealed only behind closed doors.
But what human is only pure?
Whose hands are clean in this day and age?

Surely you deserve a crown
Who is able to deny ownership of any secrets?
Not a soul I know

Home Is Where The Heart Is

Home is where the heart is, although i'm sure u know
i don't have a home, no where i can go
a house is not a home, jus a place where u can stay
itz basically a box, that you wake in every day
a home is a place, you feel comfortable and at peace
you're alwayz safe and warm, and to a home there is no key
i haven't found a home yet, that i can truly live
for i fear i will be unhappy, until i do forgive
but how could i do so? when i've lived the life i led
i spend every night, jus crying on my bed
i've wasted my life away, and it has jus barely begun
so long i have wanted, to feel the warmth of the sun
for my days are like the weather, unpredictable till it comes aroun
dreary rain or scorching sun, my days are ups and downs
i know i am supported, by those i truly need
but i don't want to be a burden, jus another mouth to feed
though for now i have a place to stay, it's not where i belong
i'm not sure why i feel this but i know that i'm not wrong
maybe i'm not supposed to be here, maybe i should be dead
but i must be wrong if i'm still here, maybe thinking too far ahead
i shouldn't have self pity, for others lives are far worse
some abused, neglected or murdered, mine is just temporarily cursed
things could get bad, and it may seem horrible rite now
but i tell u this, sympathy i won't allow
go cry for homeless people, for they had no one to care
so they end up on the streets, no food, with feet that's bare
they have no home and nor do i, but i do live in a house
now that things are in this state, i'll be quiet as a mouse
so if u find a home, please tell me where it is

so i may find my heart, and put back other pieces
for once my heart is whole, i'll be once again content
in a place i can call home, not just a room that i am lent
so all those that have given support, and have tried to help me
i wanted to let u know, i'm as thankful as can be
i know my decisions dont make u happy, my habits arent so great
but i know to be careful, so ur concern i appreciate
all your love has shown u care, it motivates me to find the pieces
of which my heart has been misplaced, afterall, *HOME IS WHERE
THE HEART IS*.....

Hodgepodge

As vision clears, one eye is opened
Not both, I can't take it all in at once.
Tell me what you see?
Because I adore not one thing
Maybe while the steam still clings to the glass
to that reflection-
You can manipulate the blur.
See what you wanna see,
think what you will,
slowly, slowly.
I spy bits and pieces to label "cute"
But I still don't like the clash
From the outside in you'd never guess
I'd rather be the spectator than the beholder
Hm... to be held, if you're that comfortable.
To love oneself in order to love another,
I'd envy her in that case.
Will you be up close and personal?
Or too close for comfort, I wonder.
Wonderful to be put at ease
Maybe it's the weather, maybe it's my mood.
No, it's just a Thursday.
Those eyes are still brown,
that shape still isn't right.
That pretty face looks pretty pissed.
Oh the joys of being a lady

Intoxication

she's a talker, she's a walker; all these guys just wanna stalk her
she's a queen, she's a dream; she's much more than she seems
intoxicologist, the ear lender; your favorite local bartender
mixing drinks, shake them through; six shots lined up for you
empty bottles, slam the glasses; make them drunk off their asses
spending money, "keep em coming"; watch them spin as they're
slumming
she's a rocker, she would knock her; tell him keep it in his dockers
just relax, have a drink; let the toxins help you think
deal with them, watch them pout; tell the bouncer throw him out
getting stupid, getting laid; someone's gotta get paid
acting legal, fake I.D.'s; stupid minors on their knees
jump in line, avoid "the scene"; what was said is what you mean
vission blurred, falling down; it's another night in town
shout out makeup, showing skin; guys wonder where you've been
taking gulps, tipping back; rookie boys that try to act
pour it long, is it green? tank it down and then you lean
sour face, pay for more; watch you fall right out the door
people laughing, having a blast; drown the issues in your past
people crawling on the bar; call a cab, leave your car
she's a hero, she's a lover; she's a hard working mother
she did her job, pay her well; saw a kiss but she won't tell
singing loud, rough the dance; if she's drunk he'll stand a chance
drop a cherry, "dry or rocks?" drunken girls who wanna box
she got talent, she's got style; piss her off and she'll go wild
she will listen, she can jam; she just won't give a damn
people sober? you're so fake. in your system till you wake
it's getting quiet, becoming dawn; work is done, she lets out a yawn
close up the club, getting on home; the tips she made would make your
mouth foam
the night is done, that enough for you? see you tomorrow, back for round
two

Not "that one"

I don't want to be that girl
The one who sways at any sign of attention
The one so desperate for affection
She would trade his gorgeous smile
For her soul, her body, her value.
I don't want to be that girl
The one in search of bended knee
The one who needs another half
Her entire appearance to lure him in
Her walk, her talk, her pretty face.
I don't want to be that girl
The one who was left at the diner alone
The one who sleeps on the bathroom floor
Her expensive mascara staining her face
She couldn't leave the mirror's side
Nor crawl over the floor, through her room, to her bed.
I don't want to be that girl
The one who sways at any sign of attention.

Pockets

How heavy is your pocket?
That small space could buy an island
Those that have money
Go through life in a shiny car
Passing by people like me,
I stand on the sidewalk and watch…
With my empty pockets.
They don't even hold your usual "button and lint"
How heavy is your pocket?
I'd love to lessen your load.
You hold that weight so well
How does it all fit?
A house, some cars, all that fine jewelry…
My pockets aren't big enough
How heavy is your pocket,
You sir, in the limo!
Today I did the unusual, unthinkable.
I chased your shiny car.
I'll go where you go, even with my empty pockets.
I'm gonna go farther.

Reality In A Nutshell

Fucked up people in this world so wasted
Secrets unfold & lies have been tasted
Surrounding ourselves with bullshit & lies
Then we get fucked over & act surprised?
Life is too short & we overload with fuckups
Working gets harder & louder are "shut up's"
Cruising, surviving, and just trying to get by
Getting left & wondering why
Everyone's corrupted whether you know it or not
Just depends if the deceptions been bought
Pictures are taken then memories erased
Broken hearts & then you're replaced
Life goes on & the sun keeps blazing
Passing off "REAL DEALS" & it's not even phasing
Fake morality & reality so clear
It all falls through when you thought you were near
Dealing with people who are all kinds of a mess
So they sabotage yours to show you who's best
Nothing they planned had turned out right
They try & try harder so you to put up a fight
The games get old & people look for lives
Some find drugs, or multiple wives
Nobody will be perfect & I tell not a lie
Don't expect unexpected, who cares if we cry
Stories have been heard & the best friend bails
Pure truth how a drunken soul never tells tales
Funny how intoxication brings out the best
They frowned upon but are ahead of the rest
We live on a rock, a speck as a state
Alcohol or weed, we can all relate
Wipe away the goals of "college & making"

If you want it, go get it, it's yours for the taking
No judging those who've been put behind bars
No one really cares, the decision isn't ours
Embrace the kind tweaker who lost to batu
Slap the religious freak that tried to judge you
Living life & seeing how it's perceived
So fucked up & relying on being relieved
Life is a bitch & then we all die
Make it a lady, something new to try
She doesn't have to be nice, just decent to seem
Make her REAL, not just what you dream
The life you live should be yours till its end
Not in the hands of who you thought was your friend
Do what you want and say what you feel
The friends that matter are the ones who've been real
Your breath is limited to fake people alike
Ignore the bark if it's stronger than the bite
Enough with the standards, why keep them so tall?
Just set us all up for a long steady fall
Take every day one by one like your last
Don't try to hide your essence or past
I'm not here to tell you what's out or what's hot
Just to prove what's real & what's not
I'm still in the process of figuring it out
Over self pity but drowning in doubt
Self esteem has never been seen so low
I stand tall for the final blow
Broken as one piece for the world to see
I have nothing to offer, just the real me.

Salt & Pepper

She has those salt and pepper locks
They travel down her spine
It reminds of her wisdom
That came with passing time
Her hair, it once was black
But that was way back when
Through peace and love and flowers
It used to twist and bend
She picks and plucks the colorless
Silently claims, "Away with you!"
Why does she pay to cover them up?
If they reflect what she's been through?
I like her salt and pepper locks
She's easier to spot among the "teens"
Age is nothing but a number
I wish I saw the tings she's seen.

Such Debris

Lately life's been all a mesh, quite a mess
With hardly time just to confess
What I mean, what I've seen,
why I've been so machine-
like all those who wander aimlessly
No purpose and no dignity
Out of sight and out of mind they say
No words could come a better day
People try to break me, fake me,
Why the need to overtake me?
Content is all you'll see of me
how hard is it to let me be?
So I walk in this void, all mine
Sleeping through days at a time
Lack of dialogue, slacking diet
A life grounded back to quiet
Multiple things have gone awry
Pitiful hands won't let her cry
An aura recedes at a steady pace
Undeserving hands have soiled this face
What ELSE has gone wrong? Well let me share with you
God dropped some issues on me, those I have one or two
Everyone knows I won't cradle my pride
who cares if it breaks? I have better qualities I hide.
As a child, I might've been 5?
My select is now denied
so what's left is not my choice
they're all oblivious to my voice
what more is there to do?

If I don't want to be like you
Am I bound to this here state
my house's own inmate?
I believe I have a brain to waste
Potential that was never chased
With all her bones stacked behind the door
and footprints ground into the floor
Many say they understand, but none can relate
Contradicting lies is all she'll taste
Once ashes sift, she'll be home free
Only then will you say you were glad to know me
The cradle will rock it's hardest, you bet
But baby won't let herself fall just yet.

As The Tide Turns

As the tide turns babies are born & people die
Many hearts yearn and old habits still try
as the tide turns they lie awake in their bed
problems resolved; good days dance in their head
as the tide turns there will always be tomorrow
the past was just another day time to look beyond the sorrow
as the tide turns children grow and learn to live
mistakes are made but we're taught "forget and forgive"
as the tide turns we'll be let down or pushed aside
make room for progression ignoring feelings that we hide
as the tide turns things tend to have an end
but life still continues wether or not you have a friend
as the tide turns lessons are taught & learned
people work to get paid; spending money we've earned
as the tide turns someone will always need a guide
life will give you obstacles. if you fail, at least you tried.

My Best Friend

Everybody loves the clubs
But me? I adore the scene.
The insane volume in a crowded room
My little slice of pie.
Eyes wide shut, hearts listening loud and clear
Watch me sway, watch me move
I'll cover every inch of the dance floor
And those songs? He plays for me.
Letting me lose myself before bed
My number one, my best friend, the DJ.

Everyone has their days
Apparently mine are every day
What's the issue for today?
Have a seat, pick your poison.
As the night wears on your voice seems softer
So I'll speak up a little
"this stool would go nicely in my kitchen"
My favorite, my best friend, the bartender.

Some people are just born a ten
Others have to work at their image
"My face could use a little TLC"
There's nothing wrong with self-improvement
I love laughter, too bad it shows
Stretch, pull, poke, and prod
I can't feel a thing!
Botox, that good stuff.
Wrinkles are no stranger to this face
Sculpting the sag and age
My priority, my best friend, the plastic surgeon.

Heartache:

"People will forget what you said. People will forget what you did. But people will never forget how you made them feel."- Maya Angelou

Don't Forget To Say Goodbye

Goodbyes were never my cup of tea
I don't even like tea, it's bitter-sweet.
But why indulge in something that isn't one or the other?
It's not sour enough to make you repeat the challenge
Nor is it sweet enough to be a treat.
Therefore, goodbye is no good.
Saying goodbye is like the end of a story
Who wants the end? No one ever does.
However, there have been seldom few I missed my chance
My gosh, how death is a greedy fool.
But on another note, some choose to leave
No goodbyes equal...
A spiraling black hole into the abyss.
When someone close to your heart leaves with no intention of return,
Your opportunity for closure or reassurance has passed,
It takes a nasty toll on your health.
Loss of appetite with a douse of insomnia,
People can't bare the sight of you without feeling pity
Your body can only weep so much
Till you begin to resemble an aimless zombie
You listen but can't hear, watch but can't see, touch but can't feel
Let's not even waste our food.
Nobody wants tea. Nobody wants goodbye.
Be that as it may, I'd choose goodbye over emptiness
Warn me before that eternal departure
Or suffer the consequences.
My pink nose and puffy eyes are sure to break your heart.
And that my friend, is non-curable with a cup of tea.

It's Like . . .

Like a menacing disease, like a soul so hard to please
Like a plague's come over me, like it just keeps torturing me
The thought of you so hard to bear, I close my eyes you're everywhere
Can't keep running, no where to hide, tearing me apart from the inside
Can't escape you, but neglecting to show, I've broken down cause you let me go
Get out of my head, leave me alone, spare my heart, and break my bones
Does it hurt to die? Cause I'm suffering in life, I won't do it, pain killers or a knife
I just can't handle this, drowning in sorrow, hoping and praying for a content tomorrow
Peers pushing me through, helping move on, wanting my feelings for you gone
Closest one's suffer, all cause my pain, hating to see me loving in vain
Sincerest regards to those who care, a foolish heart that lost a dare
My sincerest regrets to the voice within, for keeping me locked, in love with him.

LOT 1215

whats with guys and breaking my heart?
where is the joy in my world falling apart?
over my head is the theme for today
wonder what bitch broke "the fray"
analyze the meaning, obsess over the song
been waiting and waiting for so fucken long
he said he cared, and i KNOW its sincere
i guess care is limited cause he's NOT here
i was used and abused, owned and neglected
breaking my heart is a skill he perfected
she has nothing to offer but an empty bed
she'll drop him right after she gets in his head
he knew my intentions, i made them clear
he took advantage, made me think i came near
he understands cause he's felt it before
he's had his heart thrown on the floor
he must think its ok if he's not affected
just bury my heart, its been infected
disfunctional and stuck since who knows when
shoot me already, i never want to feel again.

No Strings Attached

By the owner of a lonely heart
For the people you can't tell apart
It may be caused by her late start
Or maybe it's his heavy heart?
Who's to say he won't love again?
That was never her intent anyways.
Although she cares with such intensity...
and it's not even like that.
What it must be like, he probably wouldn't know;
To have someone care unconditionally,
without expecting anything in return.
Only to be acknowledged, grateful;
No strings attached.
If I had the opportunity?
My lonely heart would ease.
To know another soul always gave me the benefit of the doubt...
Always on my defense,
Always at their own expense.
Some call it love, I call it courtesy.
While I keep your best interest at heart.
This steady pulse won't falter if I never see you again...
However, you're a sight for sore eyes.
I would breach those walls you built before I let you fade.

April 25, 2009

Who Are We?

Who am I to say you love?
Who are you to say I care?
Who am I to give my best?
Who are you to not be there?
Who am I to say you will,
When eventually you don't
Who am I to want so much,
When I have a feeling you wont?
Who am I to think you right?
Who are you to say I'm wrong?
Who am I to say you're worth?
Do you think that we belong?
Who am I to fall so fast?
Who are you to hold my trust?
Who am I to think it'll work?
Do you really believe in us?
Who am I to lower standards?
Who are you to make them high?
Who am I to be confused about you
And yet you still stay by?
Who am I to always want you
Who are you to take advantage
Who am I to always let you
Cause you only want me sometimes.
Who am I to let you do this,
Who are you to brighten my day
Why do I make it so easy for you?
I'm surprised you haven't gone your way.